Nap Tap

Written by Alexandra Wells

Illustrated by Natalia Moore

Collins

tap tap

nap nap

tap tap

nap nap

a tin

nap nap

a pan

nap nap

tap tap

tap tins

tap tin pans

tap tap tap

After reading

Letters and Sounds: Phase 2

Word count: 26

Focus phonemes: /s/ /a/ /t/ /p/ /i/ /n/

Curriculum links: PSHE: Making relationships

Early learning goals: Reading: use phonic knowledge to decode regular words and read them aloud accurately; demonstrate understanding when talking with others about what they have read

Developing fluency

- Your child may enjoy hearing you read the book.
- Encourage your child to read with expression, for example, demonstrate reading **nap** more quietly than the other words.

Phonic practice

- Say the word **tin** on page 6. Ask your child to say it too, encouraging them to sound out each letter t/i/n first, then blending.
- Repeat for the word **pans** on page 12, sounding out each letter p/a/n/s and then blending.
- Focusing on the word **pans**, ask your child to point to the letter that makes each of these sounds: /p/, /s/ and /n/.
- Look at the "I spy sounds" pages (14–15). Point to the tambourine and say: "tambourine", emphasising the /t/ sound. Ask your child to find more things in the picture that contain the /t/ sound. (e.g. *light, tomato, table, tractor, tin, teddy, TV, tap*)

Extending vocabulary

- Point to the word **tin** on page 6. Ask: What do you put in tins? (e.g. *peas, beans, spaghetti, drinks*)
- Can your child think of another word that means the same as **tin**? (*can*)
- Point to the word **pan** on page 8. Ask: What do you usually do with a pan? (e.g. *cook with it; boil potatoes in it; heat beans in it*)
- Can your child think of other things we can cook food in? (e.g. *pot, wok, casserole dish*)